GLASGOW
by night

GLASGOW NECROPOLIS, CATHEDRAL SQUARE. JOHN KNOX'S MONUMENT, ERECTED IN 1825 PRECEDING THE CEMETERY, WHICH WAS LAID OUT IN 1833, OVERLOOKS THE CITY FROM A HIGH VANTAGE POINT. THE FUMES FROM THE NEARBY BREWERY IN DUKE STREET CAN'T BE HAVING MUCH EFFECT AS HE'S REMAINED FIRMLY FIXED TO HIS PEDESTAL FOR ALL THESE YEARS.

GLASGOW
by night

DONALD CLEMENTS

LOCHAR PUBLISHING
Moffat, Scotland

Published by Lochar Publishing Ltd
MOFFAT DG10 9JU

British Library Cataloguing in Publication Data
Clements, Donald, 1945–
Glasgow by night.
1. Scotland. Strathclyde Region. Glasgow
I. Title
941.4430858

ISBN 0 948403 34 9

Acknowledgements
The author would like to thank all the city authorities, companies and
individuals without whom this book would not have been possible. A
special thank you to the citizens of Glasgow.

Design & Layout by Wide Art, Edinburgh
Typeset in Baskerville on 9/11pt by Hewer Text Composition Services
and printed in Scotland by Scotprint Ltd, Musselburgh

Dedicated to a boy-and-a-half called CHRISTOPHER.

FOREWORD

St. Mungo didn't know what he was starting away back in the year 543. His tiny settlement on the river Clyde became a city in the 12th century, and much later was described by Daniel Defoe as, 'with the exception of London, the cleanest and beautifullest and best built city in Britain'. John Betjeman enthused over the opulence and self confidence of its Victorian architecture, and many another eminent personage has given the city the nod of approbation. We've had our ups and downs of course. Our buildings long bore the dingy encrustations of industry, but are now cleaned and restored to their original glowing colours; and what would Betjeman make of the night-time splendour of the floodlit University and Kelvingrove Museum, or the grandeur of Park Circus viewed from the park?

Glasgow's self confidence was at a low ebb for quite some time, but that has changed, and this beautiful book reflects the city's growing self esteem. We all have our own images of Glasgow by night. Bridge traffic reflected in the river. Home-coming starlings whirling like black snow against a dark sky. The well refreshed wee man at the bus stop. 'Is it a song yez are wantin'?' From the air, a map of lights. The Finnieston crane against a red sunset. Raucous and sharp tongued crowds on the football terraces. **Glasgow by Night** shows us not only the places, but people. Nocturnal pleasure seekers, and those who have no home but the streets. The doctors and nurses, the policemen and women, the firemen and ambulance crews. All those who work while we sleep. In Donald Clement's superb pictures, Glasgow and its people look terrific. Surprise, surprise!

Jimmie Macgregor, Glasgow, 1990

THE TOWN AT NIGHT

The past five years or so has seen Glasgow take on a whole new dimension after dark, with the illumination of our more handsome buildings and bridges. A walk over Glasgow Bridge and along Custom House Quay, with little imagination, is not so far removed from a stroll along the Seine in Paris. The recent addition of an 'Amsterdam Type' glass-roofed motor boat, offers unsurpassed views of the river and adjacent buildings and adds further fuel to the Continental fire.

The city's Victorian architecture is a constant source of pleasure and surprise to me, from the magnificence of the City Chambers and the Mitchell Library to the humble tenement, now enjoying a new lease of life. Unfortunately the people of Glasgow lost vast amounts of their architectural heritage to the bulldozers of the fifties and sixties. St Enoch Hotel and the YMCA building in Bothwell Street, were two lamentable examples of our losses, to be replaced by cold anonymous structures of concrete, glass and steel. Thankfully our inherited architecture is going through a period of respite and conservation, and long may it continue, enabling future generations to relish our glorious past.

What of the present and future Glasgow? High rise dwellings and large sprawling housing schemes seem to be a part of our recent history which is now no longer fashionable. A high demand now exists for inner city housing, resulting in many old, and sometimes derelict, warehouses and offices being refurbished and converted, bringing a new lease of life to old and forgotten areas of the town. Merchant City is an impressive example, The Cafe Gandolfi and Babbity Bowster, two excellent hostelries in the district, ensuring life and vitality continue well into the night.

A more formal area of the city-centre is Buchanan Street pedestrian precinct, one of Glasgow's most pleasant shopping areas. The Princes Square development has ensured life goes on long after the tills have stopped ringing, as it contains several fine cafe – bars and restaurants. The Square is a fine example of modern architecture living in harmony with the old – a truly

A STARLING'S EYE VIEW OF THE CITY'S VICTORIAN SKYLINE LOOKING WEST FROM
SAUCHIEHALL STREET. IN THE NEAR DISTANCE IS TRINITY COLLEGE TOWER, WHICH
HAS RECENTLY BEEN CONVERTED TO RESIDENTIAL ACCOMMODATION. THE
UNIVERSITY SPIRE AND PARK CHURCH IS IN THE BACKGROUND.

OPPOSITE
A FAMOUS SEAT OF LEARNING, WHICH CAN BE SEEN FROM MILES AROUND
FLOODLIT OR OTHERWISE. THE GREAT TOWER OF THE UNIVERSITY, FOUNDED IN
1451, STANDS HIGH ON GILMOREHILL. ST VINCENT CRESCENT IS SHOWN IN THE
IMMEDIATE FOREGROUND.

wonderful and imaginative interior which Glaswegians must love. Whilst still retaining the original stone frontage of the old square, a futuristic building using modern materials blends flawlessly. With further development planned and the opening of the new Opera House, Buchanan Street is one part of the city with it's future secured.

The Scottish Exhibition and Conference Centre, opened in 1985, has now been partnered by the four star Forum Hotel, both built on the site of the old Queen's Dock. Voted the best exhibition centre in the world by the readers of *Conferences and Exhibitions International*, it hosts a wide range of events, including concerts from Scotland's own Hue and Cry to international stars such as Bob Dylan, and, of course, the ever popular Carnival at Christmas. Sauchiehall Street, one of the World's best known thoroughfares, offers a vast range of evening activities. Restaurants of many origins abound alongside bars, discotheques, cafes and cinemas with the odd old fashioned tearoom like 'Ma Broons' having long stood the test of time. The Willow Tearooms at number 217 is a re-creation of Charles Rennie Mackintosh's 1904 art nouveau design. After a visit here a cup of tea will never be quite the same. With the Third Eye Centre and the old Beresford Hotel, now a students residence, Sauchiehall Street is seldom quiet.

Running parallel to the famous street is the lesser known Renfrew Street, home of the city's most famous building, the spectacular Glasgow School of Art. Charles Rennie Mackintosh's masterpiece was constructed in two stages, the east wing in 1899, the west wing being added later, a true visual delight, with interiors which contain many fine details of his work. To-day Mackintosh is regarded as a genius, yet only 15 years after the completion of the school, he left Glasgow an embittered man his career in total decline ending his days (1928) on the Continent. Many other leading Glasgow architects, perhaps lesser known than Mackintosh, played a significant role in the formation of the city's skyline. Architecture of a more modern nature is the Burrell Gallery, set in the perfect surroundings of Pollok Park in the south side of the city. Opened by Her Majesty the Queen in October 1983 it houses the world famous collection which was donated to the City of Glasgow in 1944 by wealthy Glasgow shipowner Sir William Burrell. Thirty-nine years later it went on permanent display in this most impressive building.

No matter what is being achieved by the new Image Glasgow, having hopefully, at last, shed it's no mean city reputation, the populus are playing their part in the development of the transition. After all a city is nothing, day or night, without its inhabitants. Glaswegians have always been fiercely proud of their city. A sentiment, very much in evidence today.

NOW A BUSINESS CENTRE, MOST GLASWEGIANS STILL REFER TO IT AS
TEMPLETON'S CARPET FACTORY. AN ARCHITECTURAL MASTERPIECE DESIGNED BY
WILLIAM LEIPER, THE BUILDING IS SUPPOSEDLY A COPY OF THE DOGE'S PALACE IN
VENICE.

GLASGOW'S TROPICAL PARADISE IN WINTER AND SUMMER, THE KIBBLE PALACE.
ORIGINALLY BUILT AS A COULPORT BY JAMES KIBBLE, IT WAS RE-ERECTED IN THE
BOTANIC GARDENS IN 1873. THE INTERIOR, AMID THE PLANTS, CONTAINS
VICTORIAN MARBLE STATUES AND WONDERFULLY ORNAMENTAL CAST-IRON.

AN OLD LADY HAS A SEAT IN GORDON STREET, MAYBE SHE'S WAITING FOR THE
TRAVEL AGENT TO OPEN TO BOOK AN EXOTIC HOLIDAY, OR PERHAPS THE BANK
TO RENEW HER AMERICAN EXPRESS CARD. IN THE MEANTIME SHE WHILES AWAY
THE TIME BY HURTLING ABUSE AT THE PASSERS BY.

16

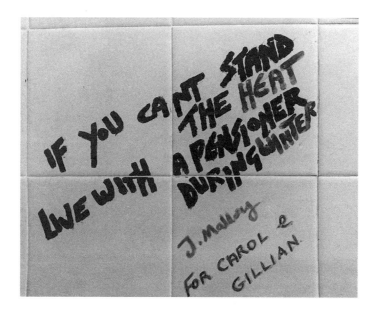

A RATHER POIGNANT PIECE OF 'MANAGEMENT APPROVED' GRAFFITI,
PHOTOGRAPHED IN PRINCES SQUARE. I WONDER IF CAROL AND GILLIAN ARE
PENSIONERS.

GEORGE SQUARE AND THE CITY CHAMBERS, THE SEAT OF LOCAL GOVERNMENT IN
THE CITY. THIS AREA HAS REMAINED VIRTUALLY UNCHANGED, BARS AND INDIAN
RESTAURANTS EXCLUDED SINCE VICTORIAN TIMES. THANKFULLY IT HAS ESCAPED
THE REDEVELOPMENT THAT HAS TAKEN PLACE IN MANY OTHER PARTS OF THE CITY.

'WHAT ON EARTH HAS SHE DONE WITH HER COIFFURE?' TWO YOUNG
THEATREGOERS DISCUSS THE MERITS OF SHAKESPEARE'S, MUCH HAIRDO
ABOUT NOTHING, IN THE FOYER OF THE CITIZEN'S.

THE RAIN GLISTENS OFF THE OLD COBBLES IN A LITTLE SERVICE LANE BEHIND
LYNEDOCH STREET – WHAT STORIES THEY COULD TELL, PHOTOGRAPHED
IN THE WEE SMALL HOURS, HENCE THE ABSENCE OF TRAFFIC. THE BRICK
BUILDING ON THE RIGHT IS THE REAR OF PARK SCHOOL.

PHOTOGRAPHED FROM A HIGH VANTAGE POINT, OVERLOOKING THE TENEMENTS OF
ANDERSON, WITH TRINITY COLLEGE TOWER IN LYNEDOCH STREET DOMINATING
THE PARK AREA SKYLINE. THE TOWER BLOCKS IN THE BACKGROUND ARE NEARBY
TO ST GEORGE'S CROSS.

AN EXCEPTIONALLY HEAVY SNOWFALL DECORATES THE ROOFS IN TRUE
CHRISTMAS CARD FASHION, FRAMED BY A GLORIOUS WINTER SKY. IT'S ALMOST
GUARANTEED THAT GLASGOW WILL BE SNOWBOUND FOR TWO OR THREE DAYS
EVERY YEAR, USUALLY IN JANUARY AND GREAT STUFF FOR THE 'WEANS'.

THE STATION-FACING ENTRANCE TO THE CENTRAL HOTEL, HOPE STREET AND GORDON STREET. THIS IMPRESSIVE BUILDING WAS ERECTED IN 1884 TO CELEBRATE THE CROSSING OF THE RIVER, AT MASSIVE COST, BY THE CALEDONIAN RAILWAY. THE INTERIOR OF THE HOTEL HAS RECENTLY BEEN REFURBISHED AND MODERNISED.

A LITTLE GIRL IS TOTALLY OBLIVIOUS TO HER MAGNIFICENT SURROUNDINGS.
SHE THINKS THIS IS JUST A BIG SWEETIE SHOP – PART OF THE TOP CHURCH IN
GLASGOW CATHEDRAL.

HIGH DUSK AT POLLOKSHAWS. ONCE A DENSELY POPULATED TENEMENTAL AREA,
THE BURGH OF POLLOKSHAWS WAS VIRTUALLY REBUILT DURING THE SIXTIES.
SEVERAL FINE EXAMPLES OF TENEMENTAL REHABILITATION CAN BE FOUND IN THE
AREA.

OPPOSITE
THE STATUE OF FIELD MARSHAL EARL ROBERTS ASTRIDE HIS STEED IN
KELVINGROVE PARK KEEPS A WATCHFUL EYE ON THE DISTANT UNIVERSITY TOWER.

THE NORTH SIDE OF BLYTHSWOOD SQUARE. THE INSERTED DOORWAY IN THE
CENTRE, NO 5, WAS DESIGNED BY CHARLES RENNIE MACKINTOSH IN 1908 FOR
THE LADY ARTISTS' CLUB. PREVIOUS TO THIS MORE SINISTER EVENTS TOOK PLACE
IN THE SQUARE. THIS IS WHERE MADELEINE SMITH SUPPOSEDLY POISIONED HER
LOVER, PIERRE EMILE L'ANGELIER, BUT A VERDICT OF NOT PROVEN WAS RETURNED.

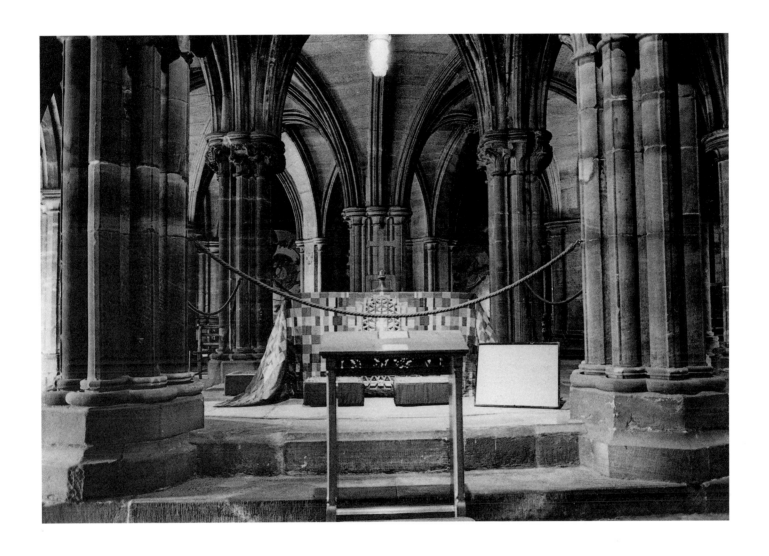

THE ELABORATELY VAULTED LOWER CHURCH OF GLASGOW CATHEDRAL,
CONTAINING ST MUNGO'S SHRINE. THIS PART OF THE CHURCH HAS
QUITE A SLOPE TO THE FLOOR ENABLING LIGHT TO ENTER FROM WINDOWS AT
THE EAST END.

A WINTER SUNSET MAKES THE IDEAL BACKDROP FOR ONE OF THE CITY'S BEST
KNOWN AND OLDEST LANDMARKS. VIEWED HERE FROM HIGH STREET, THE
TOLBOOTH STEEPLE IS A SEVEN-STORY TOWER ERECTED IN 1626 AT GLASGOW
CROSS.

OPPOSITE
THE SPECTACULAR CLYDETRUST BUILDING, LOCATED AT THE CORNER OF
BROOMIELAW AND ROBERTSON STREET. IT WAS DESIGNED BY SIR J J BURNETT WHO
WAS ALSO THE ARCHITECT FOR THAT BETTER KNOWN CITY LANDMARK CHARING
CROSS MANSIONS.

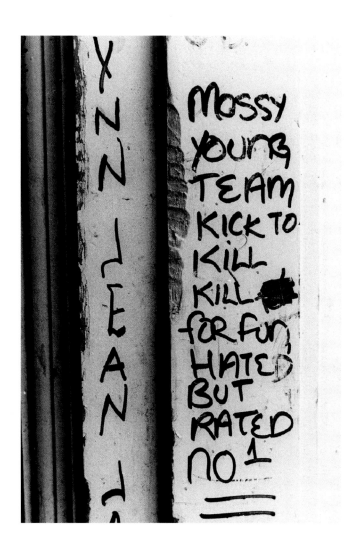

YOUNG POETS AND WOOD CARVERS ABOUND IN THE CITY, AND NO BOOK WOULD BE
COMPLETE WITHOUT SHOWING A SAMPLE OF THEIR WORK. THIS DOUBLE FEATURE
WAS DISCOVERED IN ONE OF THE LOCAL PARKS.

REPUTEDLY THE OLDEST PUBLIC HOUSE IN GLASGOW, THE SARACEN HEAD, BETTER
KNOWN IN THE LOCAL VERNACULAR AS THE 'SARI HEID' IN THE CITY'S
GALLOWGATE. NO SECURITY DOORS NEEDED ON THE CLOSES UP THIS NECK OF THE
WOODS.

OVER IN THE SOUTH SIDE OF THE CITY IS THE NEW BURRELL GALLERY, LOCATED IN
POLLOK PARK. OPENED BY HER MAJESTY THE QUEEN IN OCTOBER 1983 IT HOUSES
THE WORLD FAMOUS COLLECTION OF ART TREASURES. DONATED TO THE CITY OF
GLASGOW IN 1944 BY WEALTHY GLASGOW SHIPOWNER SIR WILLIAM BURRELL IT
WENT ON PERMENANT DISPLAY IN THIS IMPRESSIVE BUILDING 39 YEARS LATER.

AN UNUSUAL VIEW OF GLASGOW UNIVERSITY, REFLECTED IN THE TOP FLOOR
WINDOW OF THE CITY'S LATEST FOUR STAR HOTEL, THE FORUM, ON THE NEWLY
TITLED CONGRESS ROAD. THE ILLUMINATED BUILDING ON THE BOTTOM RIGHT OF
THE PHOTOGRAPH IS GOVAN TOWN HALL WITH IBROX FOOTBALL STADIUM IN THE
NEAR BACKGROUND.

A SMALL CORNER OF GLASGOW'S MOST RECENT SHOPPING COMPLEX AT ST
ENOCH SQUARE, AND A PAUSE FOR A SEAT AND A SMOKE. AN OLD GENT
REFLECTING ON HOW MUCH THE WIFE'S SPENT IN ALL THESE FANCY NEW SHOPS.

36

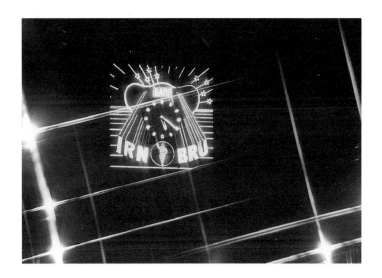

GLASGOW'S BEST KNOWN AND LOVED ADVERTISEMENT IN RENFIELD STREET.
MANY GLASWEGIANS SWEAR THIS IS THE BEST HANGOVER CURE MONEY CAN BUY.
ONCE ONLY CONSUMED LOCALLY, IT IS NOW EXPORTED TO MANY COUNTRIES
THROUGHOUT THE WORLD.

DESIGNED BY GLASGOW'S NOW FAMOUS ARCHITECT, CHARLES RENNIE
MACKINTOSH, SCOTLAND STREET SCHOOL, BUILT IN 1904. RENOVATED, CLEANED
AND FLOODLIT, IT NOW STANDS AS A REMINDER OF HIS ORIGINALITY AND
ATTENTION TO DETAIL.

OPPOSITE
GLASGOW IS FAMOUS FOR TENEMENT BUILDINGS, NOW BEING PRESERVED AND
REHABILITATED ON A GRAND SCALE, REVEALING THE WONDERFUL COLOURS AND
TEXTURE OF THE ORIGINAL STONE. THIS INTRICATE DETAIL IS ON THE CORNER OF
HAGGS ROAD AND POLLOKSHAWS ROAD, ONE OF THE FIRST TENEMENTS TO BE
REFURBRISHED AFTER THE DAMAGE CAUSED BY THE STORMS IN JANUARY 1968.

IS THAT JACK THE RIPPER LURKING ABOUT DOWN THERE? AN UNUSUALLY FOGGY
NIGHT IN GLASGOW TOWN. A STRATHCLYDE TRANSPORT BUS MAKES ITS WAY
CAUTIOUSLY ACROSS GLASGOW BRIDGE.

GETTING AROUND

Half of Scotland's five million population live in the Strathclyde Region. Glasgow, the regional capital, takes up an area of 76 square miles. Greater Glasgow extends to Renfrew, Strathkelvin, Monklands, Inverclyde and, of course, the City itself. Strathclyde Region encompasses Tobermory in the north and Girvan in the south. A vast area which is covered by most modes of transport. Buses are probably the most widespread form of transport used by the general commuter. I'm sure the old Glasgow Corporation would be turning in its grave if it could witness the chaos in Union Street and Argyle Street and since deregulation great trails of buses snake along the city's streets. Many of the newer companies are using ex-London Transport buses, and although quite ancient, it's meant the return of the conductor and conductress who can offer you change of a pound and tell you when it's time to 'geraff'. Maybe that's why some of them go by the grand title Magicbus. The facility of being able to jump off and on these buses can be extremely convenient – the chances are you're on the wrong bus owing to the distinct lack of information as to where the bus is actually going. Stories and jokes about public transport, especially the buses, play an integral part of Glasgow humour. One of my favourites is about the trainee driver who had just finished his test and the Inspector asked him some questions to assess his common sense.

'You're driving the bus up High Street and a passenger falls downstairs badly injuring himself. What would you do?'

'I'd drive into the Royal Infirmary.'

'Good thinking. You're driving along Victoria Road and a serious fight breaks out on the upper deck. What then?'

'I'd detour the bus to Craigie Street Police Station.'

'Excellent. Sitting at the terminus, two neds board your bus and menacingly inform you you're no gettin' the fare. What would you say?'

'Och, I'd tell them I'd settle for the first fortnight in August.'

For the benefit of readers not familiar with Glasgow

THIS PHOTOGRAPH PROBABLY COULD BE DESCRIBED AS AN ABSTRACT, A TERM
PERHAPS BETTER LEFT TO THE WORLD OF PAINTING. SHOT FROM AN OPEN CAR
WINDOW WHILST DRIVING ALONG THE M8 MOTORWAY HEADING WEST.

PHOTOGRAPHED FROM LONDON ROAD ON THE OUTSKIRTS OF THE EAST END, A
RAPIDLY SINKING SUN CASTS EVENING HUES ON TO THE HIGH RISE FLATS AT
SPRINGFIELD ROAD.

parley, the 'fair' is Glasgow's annual holiday taken the last two weeks in July.

For the more 'upwardly mobile' the jet aeroplane and the Golf GTI may be the choosen mode of transport. Half-an-hour after Renfrew Airport closed in May 1966, Glasgow's new airport, Abbotsinch, was operational. A mere 15-minute drive from the city centre via the M8 motorway, the airport is one of the busiest in Britain, handling over 3 million passengers annually. The hourly service to London Heathrow and Gatwick, provided by three major airlines, is the busiest route between two European cities save Paris/London.

The nucleus of Glasgow's major road system is the Kingston Bridge and the M8 Motorway. The M8 passes around the northern and western edges of the city centre, reaching Edinburgh in the east and Greenock in the West. The Kingston Bridge, opened in 1970 and consisting of two five-lane carriageways spanning 470 feet over the River Clyde, is now struggling to cope with the volume of traffic using it. Two further surface crossings are planned to run alongside the bridge, a further step in the city's comprehensive transport plan.

A guaranteed way to avoid traffic jams is to travel by the clockwork orange, Glasgow's underground. Inaugurated in 1896 as a cable-hauled system, it was electrified in 1935 by Glasgow Corporation. It is unique in being the only system in Britain which is completely run underground. It closed at the end of 1977 and was totally refurbished by Strathclyde Transport, at a cost of £60 million, re-opening in April 1980. The twin circular tracks, deposit 13 million passengers per year along its 15 stations. The service provides a heritage trail offering eight walks of discovery, each exploring from different Underground stations a separate aspect of Glasgow's heritage.

Glasgow has two major rail stations. Central in Gordon Street which opened in December 1879, has recently been refurbished with shops and restaurant facilities. A famous city meeting place, the shell, a fifteen-inch Beardmore Howitzer, has now been returned to the centre of the concourse. Central Station provides for the more southerly routes. Queen Street Station is only a short walk walk from Central, opened in February

1842 it's the oldest surviving station within the city boundary. Queen Street provides the northerly routes and a half-hourly service to Edinburgh. Both stations have suburban trains running through their low levels.

For those of a more leisurely persuasion, a fine way to get around any city is by foot and Glasgow is no exception. Three bridges cross the Clyde from the south offering a short stroll into the city centre. The most easterly is the Victoria Bridge sometimes referred to as the Stockwell Street Bridge. Moored alongside is the S V Carrick, formerly The City of Adelaide, built in 1864 and a contemporary of the Cutty Sark, she has now been transformed into the R.N.V.R. Club. Further west the Suspension Bridge crosses from Carlton Place in the south to Custom House Quay. A pedestrian bridge, spanning 414 feet, it was opened in 1851 and had a half-penny toll. The pylons, designed by Alexander Kirkland, offer a little touch of Greece to this part of town. Completing the trio is Glasgow Bridge, which crosses alongside the King George V rail bridge, going from Bridge Street in the south to Jamaica Street. By far the most spectacular way to see the city, however, is by helicopter. Familiar landscapes take on a whole new appearance and city streets become geometric patterns. Whatever way you go,
Bon voyage.

THE MITCHELL LIBRARY, NORTH STREET. THIS MAGNIFICENT STRUCTURE, NOW
OVERLOOKING THE M8 MOTORWAY, WAS NAMED AFTER THE GLASGOW TOBACCO
BARON, STEPHEN MITCHELL WHO LEFT THE MONEY TO GLASGOW FOR A PUBLIC
LIBRARY. A NON-LENDING LIBRARY, IT HOUSES VAST ARRAY OF BOOKS,
NEWSPAPERS AND PERIODICALS ON ALMOST ANY SUBJECT.

GLASGOW'S VERY OWN GRAND PRIX AT FULL THROTTLE, PHOTOGRAPHED FROM
HIGH ABOVE CHARING CROSS. HEADING EAST OR WEST YOU'RE GUARANTEED THE
THRILL OF MONZA DURING THE RUSH HOUR. THOSE WITH A DODGEY CAR OR
NERVOUS DISPOSITION OR BOTH, WOULD BE WELL ADVISED TO TAKE THE BUS.

47

ALL THE PASSENGERS WERE ON BOARD WHEN THE STEWARDESSES NOTICED
THE CAMERA. WITHOUT ANY PROMPTING FROM ME, THEY SET UP THE
PHOTOGRAPH – NATURAL POSERS, AND ALL PART OF THE SERVICE.

THE FLIGHT DECK OF A BRITISH MIDLAND BOEING 737, 300 SERIES AT GLASGOW
AIRPORT. THE CAPTAIN (LEFT) AND FIRST OFFICER MAKE THEIR FINAL CHECKS
TEN MINUTES PRIOR TO TAKE OFF EN ROUTE TO GATWICK.

A LITTLE TOUCH OF HENLEY, WITH THE BOAT HOUSE REFLECTED IN THE CLYDE.
SITUATED ON GLASGOW GREEN, IT IS INTERSPERSED BY ST ANDREW'S SUSPENSION
BRIDGE AND ALBERT BRIDGE.

THE RIVER'S MOST RECENT BRIDGE, THE FOURTEENTH TO CROSS THE CLYDE.
BELL'S BRIDGE, NAMED AFTER THE WHISKY, IS THE FIRST FOOTBRIDGE TO BE BUILT
OVER THE RIVER IN 120 YEARS. OPENED FOR THE 1988 GARDEN FESTIVAL THE
BRIDGE, AFTER SOME DOUBT, WILL REMAIN A FEATURE OF THE CITY.

THE FINNIESTON CRANE DOMINATES THE SCENE LOOKING SOUTH TOWARD THE
KINGSTON BRIDGE AND BEYOND. THE ILLUMINATED WHITE BUILDING IN THE
PICTURE, LOOKING DECIDEDLY LIKE THE MAUSOLEUM OF HALICARNASSUS, IS IN
FACT THE SCOTTISH CO-OPERATIVES FUNERAL PARLOUR IN SHIELDHALL.

PATIENTLY QUEUING FOR A BUS IN ARGYLE STREET UNDER THE CENTRAL STATION.
AFFECTIONALLY KNOWN AS THE 'HIELANMAN'S UMBRELLA,' IT WAS A ONCE
FAMOUS MEETING PLACE FOR HIGHLANDERS ON THEIR REGULAR VISITATIONS TO
GLASGOW. WITH THE ADVENT OF ONE-MAN OPERATED BUSES AND THE
DISAPPEARANCE OF THE CLIPPIES A LOT OF HUMOUR HAS GONE FROM CITY LIFE.
'THERE'S PLENTY OF SEATS UP THE STAIR,' CALLED THE IRATE PASSENGER.
'AYE,' RETORTED THE CLIPPIE, 'AN' THERE'S PLENTY O' BIG ARSES OAN
THEM'. ENOUGH TO BRING A SMILE TO ANYONE'S FACE ON A COLD MONDAY
MORNING.

GLASGOW'S UNDERGROUND, SUBWAY OR CLOCKWORK ORANGE, CALL IT WHAT
YOU WILL. PASSENGERS DISEMBARKING AT BUCHANAN STREET STATION.
INAUGURATED IN 1896 AS A CABLE-HAULED SYSTEM, IT WAS ELECTRIFIED IN 1935
BY GLASGOW CORPORATION. IT'S UNIQUE IN BEING THE ONLY SYSTEM IN BRITAIN
WHICH IS COMPLETELY RUN UNDERGROUND. IT CLOSED AT THE END OF 1977 AND
WAS TOTALLY REFURBRISHED BY STRATHCLYDE TRANSPORT, AT A COST OF £60 M,
RE-OPENING IN APRIL 1980. THE TWIN CIRCULAR TRACKS, DEPOSIT 13 MILLION
PASSENGERS PER YEAR ALONG ITS 15 STATIONS.

THE SCOTTISH CO-OPERATIVE WHOLESALE SOCIETY BUILDING IN MORRISON
STREET, SEEN HERE FLANKED BY THE KINGSTON BRIDGE. THIS BUILDING WAS
ORIGINALLY DESIGNED FOR CONSIDERATION AS THE CITY CHAMBERS IN
GLASGOW'S GEORGE SQUARE, BUT WAS NOT CHOSEN FROM THE STIFF
COMPETITION.

A WINTER SUNSET CASTS ITS SHIMMERING PINK REFLECTIONS ON THE RIVER AT
YORKHILLS QUAYS EAST BASIN. THE PUMP HOUSE IN THE FOREGROUND IS
ANOTHER FINE EXAMPLE OF RENOVATING OLD BUILDINGS. IT NOW CONTAINS
SEVERAL RESTAURANTS SERVING INTERNATIONAL CUISINE.

A HARD DAY IS OVER, SIT BACK AND RELAX, IF YOU'RE LUCKY ENOUGH TO FIND A
SEAT, AND LET THE TRAIN TAKE THE STRAIN. SOUTH-BOUND PASSENGERS WAIT
FOR THEIR TRAINS TO DEPART FROM THE UPPER LEVEL OF GLASGOW'S CENTRAL
STATION.

THIS LOWERYESQUE LOOKING SCENE IS THE CONCOURSE OF CENTRAL STATION IN
GORDON STREET. THE MAJORITY OF EYES SEEM TO BE SCANNING THE NEW
COMPUTERISED ARRIVAL AND DEPARTURE BOARD. IT'S A COMPLICATED BUSINESS
THIS TRAVELLING LARK.

THE SUSPENSION BRIDGE CROSSES THE RIVER FROM CARLTON PLACE IN THE
SOUTH TO CUSTOM HOUSE QUAY. BUILT IN 1851 AND RECONSTRUCTED IN 1871,
THIS IS CERTAINLY THE CITY'S BUSIEST FOOTBRIDGE. A SHORT STROLL OVER THE
414-FT SPAN, PASSING THROUGH THE GREEK STYLE ARCHES, TAKES YOU TO THE
HEART OF THE CITY.

OPPOSITE
MOORED NEXT TO THE VICTORIA BRIDGE, DESTINED NEVER TO SAIL AGAIN, THE OLD
SEA-GOING CLIPPER CARRICK. NOW THE R.N.V.R. CLUB SHE CATERS FOR ALL
SORTS OF OCCASIONS, WEDDING RECEPTIONS, 21ST BIRTHDAYS AND ANY EXCUSE
FOR A PARTY. A FAR CRY FROM THE DAYS WHEN SHE ROUNDED CAPE HORN.

THE DOMESTIC DEPARTURE LOUNGE AT GLASGOW AIRPORT. THE VAST MAJORITY
OF THE WEARY SOULS ARE HOLIDAY MAKERS WHO'VE BEEN HANGING AROUND
ANYTHING UP TO SIX HOURS, PATIENTLY WAITING FOR THEIR CHARTER FLIGHT TO
BE CALLED TO WHISK THEM OFF TO THE SUN. I WONDER WHAT THE AIR TRAFFIC
CONTROLLERS ARE COMPLAINING ABOUT THIS TIME.

BAGGAGE COLLECTION AT GLASGOW AIRPORT. THERE CAN ONLY BE TWO
THOUGHTS GOING ON IN THE PASSENGERS MINDS AT THIS POINT. DID THE
HANDLERS PUT MY LUGGAGE ON THE AIRCRAFT? I WONDER IF I'LL BE STOPPED
GOING THROUGH CUSTOMS?

GLASGOW'S ONLY ROUND HOUSE, OCCUPIED UP UNTIL THE LATE FIFTIES AND
SITUATED IN CROSS STREET, WHICH HAS LONG SINCE DISAPPEARED. BEAUTIFULLY
RENOVATED, WITH A NEW SLATE ROOF AND SET IN CAUSIES, A ROUNDABOUT MUST
BE A FITTING LOCATION FOR A ROUND HOUSE.

THE FLEET'S IN TOWN – A SMALL PART OF IT ANYWAY. IT IS QUITE A RARE EVENT
THESE DAYS, A SHIP DOCKED UP RIVER AS FAR AS LANCEFIELD QUAY. THE
EXCEPTION IS THE WAVERLEY, GLASGOW'S OWN LAST SEA-GOING PADDLE
STEAMER, NOW BERTHED AT ANDERSTON QUAY, READY TO TAKE THE TRIPPERS A
SAIL 'DOON THE WATTER'.

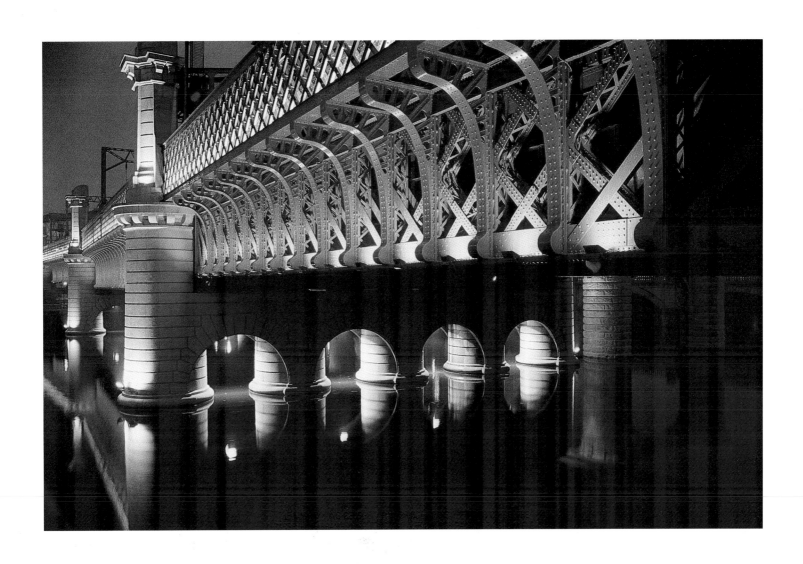

THE MIGHTY KING GEORGE V RAIL BRIDGE SPANS THE RIVER CLYDE. THE
CAREFULLY ARRANGED LIGHTING AND METICULOUS PAINTWORK SHOW THE
DETAIL OF THIS HANDSOME VICTORIAN STRUCTURE TO PERFECTION.

ONE OF THE TOWN'S 'TRENDIER BARS', DRUMMOND'S CAFE IN ST VINCENT
STREET. PREVIOUSLY THE HEAD OFFICE OF THE NOW DEFUNCT GLASGOW SAVINGS
BANK, FEATURES OF THE ORIGINAL INTERIOR ARE IN ABUNDANCE, AND ARE QUITE
SPLENDID.

LEISURE

Reflecting its status as Scotland's cultural capital and largest city, Glasgow's population of around 740,000 have a rich and cosmopolitan range of leisure and pleasure facilities available. Whatever your particular form of enjoyment may be, ballet or bingo, you'll find it in Glasgow. The city is fortunate in having a prolific selection of museums and galleries, over 35 in all. Glasgow's museums and galleries service is the largest in Britain, the collections unsurpassed in their diversity. Kelvingrove, the building of the 1901 Glasgow International Exhibition, has on permanent display a wonderful selection of paintings by Dali, Rembrant, Whistler and Turner to name a few, as well as outstanding armour, silver, glass and ceramics.

A gallery committed to the Glasgow Style, whose creator and indisputable master was Charles Rennie Mackintosh, displays many fine items of the period, including a reconstruction of the Chinese room of his Ingram Street tearooms. The People's Palace in Glasgow Green, one of the most visited musuems in Scotland, is a treasury of Glasgow's distant past. The musuem of transport, recently relocated in the Kelvin Hall, has on display a fine collection of old Glasgow trams and buses, alongside steam locomotives, which Glasgow at one time built for half the world, plus horse-drawn vehicles, early motor cars and the oldest bicycle in the world. The Hunterian Art Gallery is situated in the campus of Glasgow University, renowned for its collection of Whistler's work and an award winning reconstruction of Charles Rennie Mackintosh's own house in nearby Southpark Avenue which is decorated with his own designs and furniture. For the avant – garde the Third Eye Centre in Sauchiehall Street houses a variety of modern exhibitions complete with vegetarian food and a cafe – bar along with some very 'arty' conversation.

Glasgow hosts three international festivals, Mayfest, the Jazz and the Folk festivals. It is the home of Scottish Opera, now based at the Theatre Royal. The company, formed in 1962 has proved to be extremely popular, perhaps a touch surprising when you consider Glasgow's

'WHAT'S THAT EEJIT WITH THE CAMERA LOOKIN' AT?', OR MAYBE STRONGER THOUGHTS WERE GOING ON IN HER HEAD. THANKFULLY SHE DIDN'T INFORM ME IF THEY WERE, AS SHE ENJOYED A FAG AND A BEER IN THE TOLBOOTH BAR AT GLASGOW CROSS.

THE FIRST TEE AT HAGGS CASTLE GOLF CLUB. NO GOLFERS WERE PLAYING ON THIS
PARTICULAR DAY AS THE CLUBHOUSE HAD RUN OUT OF ORANGE BALLS. THE CLUB
HOSTED THE GLASGOW OPEN FOR SEVERAL YEARS, WHICH HAS NOW MOVED TO
GLENEAGLES AND BEEN RENAMED THE SCOTTISH OPEN. APPARENTLY THE
WEATHER'S BETTER UP THERE.

SHOT FROM THE REAR ENTRANCE OF POLLOK HOUSE, POLLOKSHAWS.
OVERLOOKING WHITE CART RIVER AND HAGGS CASTLE GOLF COURSE, A WINTER
SUNSET AND RECENT SNOWFALL SHOW THIS FINE PARKLAND AT ITS BEST.

A YOUNG CHILD LOOKS
ON IN TOTAL
BEWILDERMENT,
WONDERING WHAT ON
EARTH THIS GUY'S
DOING. THE NORTH FACE
OF THE EIGER IN MUCH
MORE COMFORTABLE
CONDITIONS, PART OF
THE FACILITIES IN KELVIN
HALL SPORT ARENA.

past. With Scottish Ballet and the Scottish National Orchestra, Orson Welles may well have chosen Glasgow as the location of The Third Man had it been filmed today, instead of Vienna. Theatre has always been popular with Glaswegians, though some English comedians might not agree, and the City's theatres offer a diversity of productions from pantomime and comedy to innovative works especially from the Citizens', and the Tron.

The name Glasgow is derived from the Gaelic for 'the dear green place', a fitting title for a city with more green open space than any other city region in Britain. It boasts over 70 parks offering an exceptionally wide range of facilities including putting, tennis, the swings and roundabouts, football pitches, bowling green and boating ponds. It's surprising Glasgow hasn't produced a famous mariner – perhaps the male population were too engrossed sailing their model boats in the parks. As a photographer I could spend many pleasant hours capturing images of the parks and the buildings within. The Botanic Gardens has been on its present site since 1842, the focus of attention being the Kibble Palace, which contains a fabulous collection of tropical plants interspaced with marble statues and ornamental ponds. Gifted to the city by the Maxwell family, Pollok Country Park has within its grounds the superb 18th century mansion Pollok House, furnished in the style of the period and displaying paintings by El Greco and Goya among others – the snooker table is not for hire.

Not everyone is interested in the cultural side of life and a visit to a museum or art gallery for some could be equated to a dental appointment or an afternoon with your mother-in-law. I was informed recently by a patron in a city pub that he was 'totally pissed aff wi' awe this culture crap, whit's in it fur me?' Don't despair, there's much more to Glasgow.

If the speculative exhilaration of the toss of the dice or turn of a card is your speciality, the city can offer several casinos all willing and eager to take your bets. Greyhound racing in Shawfield Stadium offers the gambler a more traditional form of betting. Since 1872 when Scotland first played England, football has been Glasgow's passion, especially with the famous double act,

68

Rangers and Celtic. Golf, invented by the Scots, is now almost as popular as our national sport, with around 130 courses all within an hour's drive from Glasgow, including the world renowned Gleneagles, host of the Scottish Open, and the Ayrshire coast, with the championship links of Troon and Turnberry. The city has a vast array, private and public, of indoor sports facilities catering for most activities from badminton to billiards.

With all this diverse and cosmopolitan entertainment available in the city, a few pints and a fish supper, or one of the many variations available, still remains the most popular night on the town. Pubs, lounge bars, bistros and even a few cocktail bars, offering everything from a hauf an' a hauf to a tequila sunrise are plentiful. In the city you can eat in a different country every night. All tastes are catered for, and all tastes are welcomed by the city dweller. Glasgow even has its own red light district, dotted here and there with a few massage parlours – not quite the Reeperbahn, but Glasgow. All in all a great city which can look forward to an even greater future.

A BREAK FOR A BURGER AT GLASGOW GREEN. NOT SO LONG AGO THE ONLY TAKE
AWAY FOOD AVAILABLE IN GLASGOW WAS THE EVER POPULAR FISH SUPPER, NOW
CARRY OUTS HAVE BECOME A WAY OF LIFE – NOT ONLY THE LICENSED VARIETY,
BUT EVERYTHING FROM KASHMIRI CHICKEN TO KEBABS.

LEADED GLASS PANELS DECORATE THE WINDOWS OF THE HORSESHOE BAR IN
DRURY STREET, ADVERTISING THE FACT THAT ONCE THROUGH THE DOORS YOU
WON'T BE DRINKING SASPORILLA. VERY MUCH A TRADITIONAL PUB, ADORNED WITH
VICTORIAN GRANDEUR AND OPULENCE.

THE GLASGOW BASED SCOTTISH BALLET AT VARIOUS STAGES OF REHEARSAL ON
STAGE AT THE THEATRE ROYAL. FOUNDED IN 1969, THE COMPANY CONSISTS OF
SOME 46 DANCERS OF MANY NATIONALITIES INCLUDING SCOTLAND ITSELF.
SCOTTISH BALLET HAS PERFORMED IN MANY COUNTRIES THROUGHOUT THE
WORLD, AS FAR AFIELD AS AUSTRALIA AND THE UNITED STATES OF AMERICA. MANY
CELEBRATED DANCERS HAVE APPEARED WITH THE COMPANY THROUGHOUT THE
YEARS, INCLUDING RUDOLF NUREYEV, DAME MARGOT FONTEYN AND NATALIA
BESSMERTNOVA. THE COMPANY HAS ITS OWN FULLY EQUIPPED STUDIO THEATRE
IN WEST PRINCESS STREET WHERE A VARIETY OF WORKS ARE PRESENTED
THROUGHOUT THE YEAR.

ACTRESSESS OF FABLEVISION THEATRE COMPANY CAREFULLY APPLY THEIR
MAKE-UP BEFORE A PERFORMANCE.

THE COMPANY PERFORMING A SCENE FROM *WITCH HUNT* ON STAGE AT THE
TRON THEATRE.

FABLEVISION IS A NEW AND EXITING THEATRE COMPANY PRODUCING
MULTI-THEATRE WITHIN THE BROAD SPECTRUM OF ENTERTAINMENT.
FABLEVISION'S WORK ENCOMPASSES ALL AGE GROUPS AND, WITHIN THAT, THE
DISADVANTAGED AND THE INDIVIDUAL. FABLEVISION ACTS AS A CATALYST WITHIN
THE COMMUNITY FOR EDUCATIONAL DEVELOPMENT, ENHANCED COMMUNICATION
AND CREATIVE PARTICIPATION. THE COMPANY IS UNIQUE, IN THAT IT IS THE ONLY
SCOTTISH COMPANY CREATING THEATRE SPECIFICALLY SUITABLE FOR
MIXED-ABILITY AUDIENCES WHICH ALL MEMBERS OF THE COMMUNITY CAN ENJOY
TOGETHER.

73

THE OLD STAG BAR IN GREENVIEW STREET. IT IS A LOCAL IN THE TRUE SENSE, AS
IT'S USED MAINLY BY THE RESIDENTS OF POLLOKSHAWS. THE CUSTOMERS IN THIS
BAR ARE OFFERED TO BREAK THE SEALS BEFORE THE BARMAN PROFERS THE
BOTTLE TO AN OPTIC, SO WHEN YOU ASK FOR A BELLS

74

MULTI-STOREY TOWER BLOCKS DOMINATE THE EAST-END SKYLINE, WHILE
TENNENT'S CALEDONIAN BREWERY IN DUKE STREET CONTINUES ITS PROCESS.
PARKHEAD STADIUM, HOME OF CELTIC FOOTBALL CLUB, IS IN THE BACKGROUND.

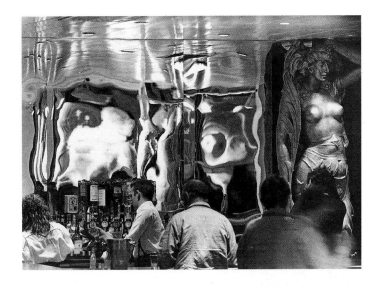

THE CITIZENS' THEATRE, IN GORBALS STREET FIRST OPENED IT'S DOORS IN 1878 AS
THE ROYAL PRINCESS THEATRE. AN ORIGINAL LEADED GLASS WINDOW PANEL
SURVIVES FROM THE PERIOD, AND IS NOW DISPLAYED IN THE FOYER. IT WAS
RE-NAMED THE CITIZENS' IN 1945. THE STATUES, WHICH ONCE ADORNED THE ROOF
OF THE BUILDING, REPRESENT THE FOUR GREEK MUSES – MUSIC, DRAMA,
TRAGEDY AND DANCE. THE LADY WITH THE GREAT FIGURE TO THE RIGHT OF THE
FOYER BAR, IS ONE OF FOUR SURVIVORS FROM THE OLD PALACE THEATRE, WHICH
USED TO BE NEXT DOOR. NICKNAMED A 'NOUTCH GIRL' SHE REPRESENTS AN INDIAN
WARRIOR DANCER. THE THEATRE COMPLETED IT'S REFURBISHMENT PROGRAMME
IN MAY 1989.

FAIRGROUND
ATTRACTIONS AT
GLASGOW GREEN ON A
RAINSOAKED 5TH
NOVEMBER. THE OTHER
TRADITIONAL TIME FOR
THE 'SHOWS' IN
GLASGOW IS THE FAIR
HOLIDAY, HELD DURING
THE LAST TWO WEEKS IN
JULY.

A POPULAR PLAYGROUND IS THE LEISURE POOL IN POLLOK'S COWGLEN ROAD, LONG OVERDUE IN THE AREA. ONE OF THE NICEST POOLS IN THE CITY, PROVIDING A GREAT DAY OUT FOR ALL THE FAMILY, ESPECIALLY THE DADS, AS IT HAS A VERY PLEASANT LITTLE LOUNGE BAR WHERE YOU CAN SAFELY KEEP AN EYE ON THE KIDS FROM THE REFLECTION ON YOUR PINT.

THIS WAS SCOTLAND'S FINAL CHANCE TO GAIN THE ONE POINT REQUIRED TO TAKE THEM THROUGH TO THE WORLD CUP FINALS IN ITALY 1990. IN FRONT OF A 63,987 CROWD AT HAMPDEN PARK, THEY EARNED THE REQUIRED POINT. AS USUAL THE TEAM DID JUST AS MUCH AS THEY HAD TO AND GAVE EVERYONE HEART FAILURE WITH A 1-1 DRAW AGAINST NORWAY.

HALF-TIME ENTERTAINMENT, AND A CHANCE FOR A FEW OF THE LADS TO SAY THEY HAVE PLAYED AT HAMPDEN.

THE GAME'S OVER, AND AS IS USUAL AFTER A HARD BATTLE, THE ARMY IS RAVENOUS. HOT DOGS AND BURGERS ARE IN PLENTIFUL SUPPLY OUTSIDE THE STADIUM.

80

NOT THE ONE-ARMED VARIETY, BUT BANDITS JUST THE SAME. PUNTERS CHANCE
THEIR LUCK IN AN AMUSEMENT ARCADE IN ARGYLE STREET. THREE BARS WOULD
DO NICELY.

DEEPLY ENGROSSED STUDYING THE CARD AT SHAWFIELD DOG TRACK – WELL,
SOMEONE HAS TO PICK A WINNER. THE RACES ARE RUN EVERY TUESDAY,
THURSDAY AND SATURDAY. ONCE THE HOME GROUND OF CLYDE FOOTBALL CLUB,
THE STADIUM NOW HOSTS SPEEDWAY RACING DURING THE SUMMER MONTHS.

THE BOOKIES HERE WERE ALL SMILES AND INTERESTED IN THE CAMERA PRIOR TO
THE PUNTER ARRIVING WITH A WAD OF TENNERS – THE HARE WOULD HAVE BEEN
IMPRESSED AT THE SPEED THE CASH DISAPPEARED INTO THE BAG. A FAMOUS
GLASGOW INSTITUTION THE 'DUGS' AT SHAWFIELD STADIUM.

OPPOSITE
REMEMBER, REMEMBER THE 5TH OF NOVEMBER. THE SPLENDID FIREWORK
DISPLAY AND FAIRGROUND ATTRACTIONS ON GLASGOW GREEN ARE AN ANNUAL
EVENT, COURTESY OF GLASGOW DISTRICT COUNCIL.

A SMALL PICTURE HOUSE IS PART OF THE 1938 STREET RE-CONSTRUCTED IN THE MUSEUM OF TRANSPORT, IN THE CITY'S KELVIN HALL. COMPLETE WITH COBBLES, VINTAGE CARS AND A SUBWAY CARRIAGE AND STATION. MODELLED ON MERKLAND STREET, IT IS A DELIGHTFUL EXPERIENCE FOR ADULTS AND CHILDREN ALIKE.

A LONE SPECTATOR KEEPS AN EYE ON THE ATHLETICS TRACK, PERHAPS DREAMING SHE MIGHT WIN A RACE DOWN THERE ONE DAY. MAYBE SHE ALREADY HAS, AND IS NOW CONTEMPLATING BIGGER AND BETTER THINGS, SCOTTISH CHAMPION, EUROPEAN ATHLETE OF THE YEAR, OLYMPIC GOLD, THERE AGAIN MAYBE'S SHE'S JUST IN THE HUFF.

THE POT STILL BAR IN HOPE STREET OFFERS FROM ITS GANTRY THE FINEST
SELECTIONS OF MALT WHISKIES IN TOWN. IF THEY DON'T STOCK YOUR
PARTICULAR TIPPLE, WHICH IS UNLIKELY, THEY'LL ORDER IT IN FOR YOU. WHAT'S
THIS GUY DOING DRINKING A PINT?

THEY'RE OFF! THE SELECTION HAS BEEN MADE, THE BETS HAVE BEEN PLACED, THE
HARE'S GOING FLAT OUT AND THE TRAPS FLY OPEN. AFTER A LAP AND A HALF OF
NAIL BITING TENSION THE RACE IS OVER AND THE DOGS MOMENTARILY POUNCE ON
THEIR PREY. SOME SMILE, SOME SIGH, SOME GROAN, TORN UP BETTING SLIPS
ABOUND, THEN IT'S BACK TO THE CARD TO STUDY FORM FOR THE NEXT RACE.
BOUND TO PICK A WINNER THIS TIME.

USUALLY THE MOST INTERESTING TRADITIONAL PUBS ARE TO BE FOUND ON
CORNERS AND THE GRIFFEN BAR IS NO EXCEPTION, LOCATED AT BATH STREET
AND ELMBANK STREET. THE ETCHED GLASS AND WOOD OF THE EXTERIOR ARE
QUITE SPECIAL. FORMERLY KNOWN AS THE KING'S ARMS, A STRANGER ASKING A
KNOWLEDGEABLE GLASWEGIAN WHERE THE KING'S ARMS WAS, USUALLY
RECEIVED THE REPLY, 'ROUND THE QUEEN'S A—.'

THE 'SARI HEID' HAS QUITE A REPUTATION FOR BEING A BIT ON THE ROUGH SIDE – WINE, CIDER AND SAWDUST. IMAGINE MY SURPRISE ON WITNESSING THIS SCENE, A QUIET GAME OF CHESS ON TOP OF THE BAR. NO DOUBT THE THINKING MAN'S PUB.

THERE MUST HAVE BEEN A LONGISH WALK BETWEEN HIS LAST PUB AND THE NEXT. PERHAPS HE'S A TOUCH DISORIENTATED AND HAS LOST THE SEQUENCE OF THE CRAWL. A LITTLE INTERRUPTION IN THE EVENINGS PROCEEDINGS – OBVIOUSLY IN HIS CASE URGENTLY NECESSARY.

LAST ORDERS IN THE GEORGIC BAR, SHAWLANDS. A LAST BASTION OF MALE
CHAUVINISM, THERE'S NO LADIES TOILET, BUT FEMALES, YOUNG AND OLD, ARE
KNOWN TO FREQUENT THE BAR AND HAVE A DRINK OR TWO. I DOUBT IF THEY COULD
STAY FOR MORE.

THE OLD TOLL BAR, SITUATED AT PAISLEY ROAD TOLL HAS BECOME QUITE FAMOUS
THESE DAYS. USED FREQUENTLY BY TELEVISION TO FILM BEER COMMERCIALS, IT IS
A GRAND OLD PUB WITH PROBABLY THE FINEST GANTRY IN GLASGOW.

ALEXANDER 'GREEK' THOMSON'S ST VINCENT STREET CHURCH, BUILT IN 1859.
BEAUTIFULLY RENOVATED AND FLOODLIT, THE BUILDING IS VERY SIMILAR TO
CALEDONIA ROAD CHURCH, WHICH UNFORTUNATELY HAS FALLEN INTO A STATE OF
DISREPAIR. HOPEFULLY IT WILL SOON BE BROUGHT UP TO A SIMILAR STANDARD.

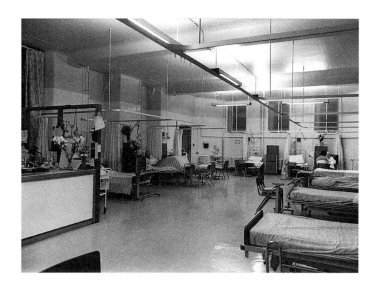

A QUIET MOMENT ON A WARD OF GLASGOW'S ROYAL INFIRMARY IN CASTLE STREET
GIVES THE NIGHT STAFF NURSE AN OPPORTUNITY TO WRITE UP HER NOTES.

NIGHT WORKERS

Making use of the roads or public transport in and around Glasgow during the morning and evening rush hours it is self-evident that the vast majority of people fortunate enough to be in regular employment work the hours nine to five. Traffic is at a standstill, be it on the motorway or a familiar shortcut, everybody seems to be using the same side streets. Buses and trains are at their busiest and the pavements throng with pedestrians. The city is very much awake and on the move.

Some 400,000 people work in the city, with the best part of those employed during the day, doing so-called regular hours and leading a 'normal lifestyle' – eating and playing with the children, enjoying the city nightlife, watching peak time television, sleeping when it's quiet. This is a way of life the majority of us take for granted. Glasgow, like all large cities, is never totally asleep. A vast array of people work long into the night and beyond. Once the office door is closed, some form of entertainment could be called for, a simple drink after a hard day, a meal before the theatre, the cinema and perhaps, for the more energetic, off to a disco or a concert. And if that is not sufficient, the casinos are open till 4 am. With the night's winnings safely tucked away, it's into a taxi for home, just a simple night out which would be impossible without the waiters, barmen, performers, doormen, taxi drivers – a seemingly endless list of night workers providing essential services we all take as the norm.

In the course of this project I found myself on several occasions driving around the city centre between midnight and 6 am. I was quite astonished by the activity going on in the streets. Road sweepers were much in evidence sprucing up the gutters and pavements ready for the next day. The lone policeman on his beat, torch flashing, checking premises were lockfast and secure. The first edition of the morning papers being delivered to the newsagents to be prepared for the long suffering paper-boy and the earliest commuter. By about 4.30 am, milk lorries and bakers vans start their busy schedule of deliveries, then it's the turn of the buses arrriving in town with the early starters. Hordes of females young and old

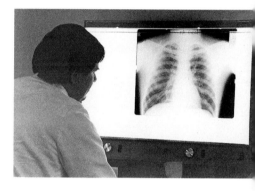

A DOCTOR IN THE
ACCIDENT EMERGENCY
DEPARTMENT CHECKS
HIS PATIENT'S CHEST
X-RAY.

AN INTERIOR GLIMPSE OF STIRLING'S LIBRARY IN ROYAL EXCHANGE SQUARE.
FORMERLY OCCUPIED BY THE ROYAL BANK OF SCOTLAND, IT NOW HOUSES BOOKS
OF A MUCH MORE INTERESTING AND SCHOLARLY NATURE.

FRASER'S DEPARTMENT STORE, DECORATED FOR CHRISTMAS, IN BUCHANAN
STREET'S PEDESTRIAN PRECINCT. A PLEASANTLY OLD-FASHIONED SHOP, SELLING
THE VERY LATEST MERCHANDISE AND SERVICES, EVERYTHING FROM A
CHESTERFIELD SUITE TO CHIROPODY CAN BE PURCHASED HERE. A TRUE
SHOPPERS' PARADISE.

descend on the streets to prepare and clean the offices, ready for a new day's trading. Postmen making their way through George Square towards the General Post Office to collect the mail for the first delivery. This small sample seen on the streets is only a fraction of work going on during the night. A vast army are busy behind closed doors. The essential services must be manned and ready for action twenty-four hours a day. The police, fire brigade and amublance service must be able to provide a fast and efficient service throughout the night – crime, fire, accidents and emergencies don't keep regular hours. Anything from a cut finger to a coronary, the city's hospitals are prepared for the nights casualties, or babies wanting delivered.

Who would think twice about picking up a telephone and calling the operator at 4 am, asking to be put through to Central Station or Glasgow Airport to inquire about the departure and arrival times of trains and planes. These are driven and flown by crews who work long into the night, taking the business traveller or holiday maker all over Britain, Europe and beyond – taxi drivers, hotel receptionists, porters and kitchen staff all patiently wait to provide a service.

Less often seen by the general public are the night shift workers. Factories, engineering works, steel works and breweries all produce the necessities of life from a loaf of bread to beer. Normally the workers in these industries work the three shift system. The early shift six to two, the back shift two to ten and of course, the night shift ten to six. How many of us could adjust to this way of life? I wonder if they had the choice would they settle for nine to five – perhaps not. The pleasure of quiet roads, easy parking and a guaranteed seat on the buses and trains are considerable advantages over the hard pressed commuter starting between eight and nine, with perhaps the added frustration of dropping the children off at school. Murder polis!

The domestic problems of night workers are considerable. The harassed wife tries to keep under fives reasonably quiet while the husband attempts to get his obligatory eight hours, interrupted no doubt by traffic sounding horns and people ringing the door bell. Add to this irregular meal times and having to arrange babysitters –

THE AMBULANCE CREW HAVING SAFELY TRANSFERRED THEIR PATIENT PERPARE FOR ANOTHER CALL IN THEIR BUSY SCHEDULE.

nobody said earning a living was easy. Unfortunately, as in most cities and towns in Britain, Glasgow being no exception, the level of unemployment is unacceptably high and given the opportunity the majority of jobless would work the most unsociable hours.

A STRANGE NAME FOR A CAR WASH. ACCORDING TO THE ATLAS, IMO IS A STATE IN SE NIGERIA – A LONG WAY TO GO TO GET YOUR CAR CLEANED. MAYBE IT'S JUST A FRIENDLY REMINDER INFORMING US TO COME IN MORE OFTEN.

NOW A RESTAURANT AND WINE BAR, THE NORTH ROTUNDA WAS THE ENTRANCE TO
THE RIVER CLYDE'S FIRST TUNNEL, USED MAINLY FOR PEDESTRIAN AND
HORSE-DRAWN VEHICLES. STANDING GUARD OVER IT IS THAT OTHER ENGINEERING
MASTERPIECE, THE MASSIVE FINNIESTON CRANE, WHICH IS STILL IN USE TODAY.

I VERY MUCH DOUBT IF GEORGE FORMBY WOULD BE PLAYING HIS UKULELE IF HE WAS SUSPENDED FROM THIS FLIMSY PIECE OF APPARATUS. STILL, I SUPPOSE HE NEVER GOT HIGHER THAN TWO STOREYS. HAVE WINDOW CLEANERS NEVER HEARD OF VERTIGO? THE CRADLE PHOTOGRAPHED HERE IS AT THE TOP OF THE EIGHTEEN FLOOR FORUM HOTEL.

A SENIOR REPORTER ON THE NIGHT NEWS DESK, LOOKING A TOUCH HARD PRESSED, GATHERS INFORMATION FOR HIS ARTICLE.

A CASEROOM COMPOSITOR PREPARES THE FRONT PAGE MAKE-UP AS DEADLINE TIME APPROACHES FOR THE FIRST EDITION.

THE 27TH JANUARY 1783 SAW THE VERY FIRST EDITION OF THE GLASGOW HERALD, KNOWN THEN AS THE GLASGOW ADVERTISER. IN 1980 THE PAPER MOVED INTO THE AGE OF VDU'S AND COMPUTERS WHEN IT LEFT MITCHELL STREET FOR TODAYS HI-TECH PREMISES IN ALBION STREET. THE NEWSPAPER CURRENTLY HAS A CIRCULATION OF AROUND 125,000 DAILY SALES.

PRINTED NEWS-SHEETS SPEEDILY MAKE THEIR WAY TO THE FOLDER OPERATION.

MODERN ARCHITECTURE AT ITS VERY FINEST, LINKING THE OLD WITH THE NEW.
PRINCES SQUARE IN BUCHANAN STREET IS ONE OF THE MOST RECENT AND
SUCCESSFUL NEW SHOPPING MALLS TO APPEAR. A CONTINENTAL ATMOSPHERE
PREVAILS WITH CAFE-BARS, COFFEE SHOPS AND RESTAURANTS.

AN EERIE LOOKING NIGHT ON GLASGOW GREEN. A COMBINATION OF MOONLIGHT
AND, NOT QUITE AS ROMANTIC SOUNDING, ELECTRICITY, BRIGHTLY ILLUMINATING
THE LONG JOHN INTERNATIONAL DISTILLERY IN MOFFAT STREET – THE CREATION
OF THE WATER OF LIFE DOES NOT STOP JUST BECAUSE IT GETS DARK.

THE FINISHED NEWSPAPER BEING CONVEYED TO DESPATCH, WHERE THEY WILL BE
COUNTED, LABELLED, INVOICED AND DELIVERED THROUGHOUT THE COUNTRY.

THE FINAL STAGE IN THE PROCESS, A 4 AM DELIVERY TO WILLIAM PORTEOUS IN
ROYAL EXCHANGE PLACE.

AFFECTIONATELY KNOWN AS THE ANNEX, THE PRESS BAR, CONVENIENTLY
SITUATED BETWEEN THE HERALD AND EVENING TIMES OFFICES, RELIEVES THE
RIGOURS OF A HARD NIGHT'S WORK.

THE OLD REFLECTED IN THE NEW. ST COLUMBA'S CHURCH IN ST VINCENT
STREET, MIRRORED IN THE GLASS PANELS OF A MOST RECENT ADDITION TO THE
SKYLINE – THE BRITOIL BUILDING, A MASSIVE STRUCTURE WHICH STRETCHES
DOWN PITT STREET TO BOTHWELL STREET.

LOOKING SADLY IDLE, THE CRANES OF GOVAN SHIPYARD TOWER OVER THE PARISH
CHURCH OF THAT NAME. GOVAN WAS AT ONE TIME A NAME SYNONYMOUS WITH
SHIPBUILDING GOING BACK 150 YEARS. TIME MARCHES ON AND MANY NEW AND
ENTERPRISING BUSINESSES HAVE NOW COMMENCED IN THIS AREA OF THE CITY.
THE GLENIFFER BRAES ON THE OUTSKIRTS OF PAISLEY ARE IN THE FAR
BACKGROUND.

THE NIGHT WATCH OF STRATHCLYDE FIRE BRIGADE PUT THEMSELVES AND THEIR
EQUIPMENT THROUGH A RIGOUROUS TRAINING SESSION AT POLMADIE STATION,
COMPLETE WITH BREATHING APPARATUS, HIGH EXPANSION FOAM AND WATER
TENDER – A WELL-TRAINED AND VERY CLEAN FIRE-FIGHTING UNIT.

A WELDER BEGINS HIS NIGHT SHIFT AT WEIR PUMPS OF CATHCART, JUST ONE OF
THE MANY TRADES REQUIRED TO KEEP THIS OLD ESTABLISHED ENGINEERING
COMPANY RUNNING SMOOTHLY AND EFFICIENTLY.

THE DYING RAYS OF A WINTER SUN CAST THEIR LIGHT ON A MONUMENTAL STATUE
OF CHRIST AND THE CROSS. ST PETER'S CEMETERY, DALBETH.

OPPOSITE
GLASGOW IS INDEED FORTUNATE IN HAVING TWO CATHEDRALS. PICTURED HERE IS
PROBABLY THE LESSER KNOWN, ST ANDREW'S IN CLYDE STREET AND
APPROPRIATELY REFLECTED IN THE WATERS OF THAT RIVER.

THE TELLERS HAVE ALL GONE HOME. NO DOUBT THE DAY WILL HAVE SEEN SOME
HAPPY CUSTOMERS, ALONG WITH A FEW DISGRUNTLED ONES. AT LEAST WE CAN BE
CONSOLED IN THE KNOWLEDGE OUR LOANS AND OVERDRAFTS ARE BEING KEPT
SPICK-AND-SPAN. AFTER SHE'S POLISHED THE FLOOR MAYBE SHE WILL LAUNDER
SOME MONEY.

WORKING LATE AT THE OFFICE. THERE ARE SOME 16,000 COMPANIES IN GLASGOW
EMPLOYING 400,000 PEOPLE, MAKING IT THE COMMERCIAL CAPITAL OF
SCOTLAND. WITH HEAVY INDUSTRIES IN DECLINE GLASGOW HAS DIVERSIFIED
ADMIRABLY TO THE WORLD OF HIGH TECHNOLOGY AND THE SERVICE INDUSTRIES.

TERRY, THE TATTOO ARTIST OF CHISHOLM STREET, DOES SOME CAREFUL PRICKING
AND STAINING TO HIS CLIENTS FOREARM. TERRY'S A MAN OF MANY WORDS, A
TACTIC DEVISED, PERHAPS, TO KEEP THE RECIPIENTS MIND OFF THE PAIN.

PART OF THE BOTTLING HALL OF JAMES BURROUGH DISTILLERS IN LONDON ROAD.
LONG JOHN, BLACK BOTTLE, ISLAY MIST, TORMORE AND LAPHROAIG ARE SOME OF
THE FAMOUS BRAND NAMES PRODUCED BY THE COMPANY.

IF ONLY THE M8 WERE LIKE THIS DURING THE DAY. CONSTRUCTION WORKERS ON
THE INFAMOUS BRIDGE THAT GOES NOWHERE. OVER THE YEARS MANY SCHEMES
HAVE BEEN PUT FORWARD REGARDING THIS FOLLY – NIGHTCLUBS, RESTAURANTS
AND CASINOS TO NAME BUT FEW. ALAS. NOW WE KNOW ITS FATE, ANOTHER
BORING OFFICE BLOCK.

OPPOSITE
GLASGOW CATHEDRAL, CATHEDRAL SQUARE, BUILT DURING THE LATE 12TH
CENTURY ONWARDS. DEDICATED TO ST MUNGO, THE CITY'S PATRON SAINT, THE
CATHEDRAL IS ONE OF THE OLDEST GOTHIC STYLE CHURCHES IN SCOTLAND. NOW
A TOURIST ATTRACTION, IT IS STILL USED FOR PRESBYTERIAN WORSHIP.

A NEW GENERATION TYPE 23 ANTI-SUBMARINE FRIGATE, UNDER CONSTRUCTION AT
YARROW SHIPBUILDERS LIMITED, SCOTSTOUN. HMS LANCASTER, CAPABLE OF 27
KNOTS, IS THE THIRD OF THREE SUCH WARSHIPS TO BE BUILT BY THE YARD.

BRITISH STEEL'S CLYDEBRIDGE IRONWORKS, MOTHERWELL. GLASGOW AT ONE
TIME DID HAVE IT'S OWN IRONWORKS, QUITE A FAMOUS ONE AT THAT, DIXON'S
BLAZES IN THE GORBALS, WHICH CLOSED IN THE LATE FIFTIES. LITTLE CHILDREN IN
THE AREA KNEW OF IT WELL. WHEN MISBEHAVING, THEY WERE THREATENED WITH
BEING SENT TO THE 'BIG BAD FIRE'. WHEN REALLY BAD THEY WERE TOLD IT WAS
STOKED BY THE DEVIL. I DOUBT TODAYS KIDS WOULD SWALLOW THAT LOT.

GIRL WAITING. I TOOK A PHOTOGRAPH, SHE TOOK THE P**S

IN THE GLASGOW OF YESTERYEAR, A DONNER MEANT GOING FOR A SHORT STROLL.
MENTION THE WORD NOW AND KEBABS ARE THE ORDER OF THE DAY, A FAIRLY
RECENT ADDITION TO THE RECIPIENT PALATE OF THE CITY. OUTER MONGOLIAN
RESTAURANT'S, CAN'T BE TOO FAR OFF.

A TRAFFIC DEPARTMENT RANGE ROVER, PARKED ON THE HARD
SHOULDER OF THE WEST STREET APPROACH RAMP, KEEPS A VIGILANT EYE ON THE
EVER BUSY KINGSTON BRIDGE.

MOUNTED POLICEMEN PATROL THE PERIMETER OF HAMPDEN PARK AFTER THE
SCOTLAND-NORWAY INTERNATIONAL. THE HORSES SHOW SOME FANCY
FOOTWORK AND ARE IMMEDIATELY PUT ON THE SUBS' BENCH.